La lisière   **au bord**   *le mur*

la séparation au bout la    ion

à la fin   la limite   e

de l'autre côté   *à l'extrémité*

La lisière   **au bord**   *le mur*

la séparation au bout la frontière   la ligne de démarcation

à la fin   la limite   **la bordure**

de l'autre côté   *à l'extrémité*

Traverser passer franchir essayer **rallier**

rejoindre venir se rendre *se faufiler* s'effacer

transiter *changer* disparaître ***marcher*** s'en aller

fuir *quitter*

se glisser laisser tenter

Traverser *passer* franchir essayer **rallier**

rejoindre venir se rendre *se faufiler* s'effacer

transiter *changer* disparaître ***marcher*** s'en aller

fuir *quitter*

se glisser laisser tenter

but it's a long way

ATROX
that which cannot be eaten
:
an occasional series of works
published by Nightboat Books

but it's a long way

frédérique guétat-liviani

translated by nathanaël

Nightboat Books
New York

mais ça fait loin was first published in 2017 in a portfolio of works under the title *la porte rouge* and jointly published by Fidel Anthelme X (Marseille) and L'Antre Lieux (Avignon). *la porte rouge* is comprised of texts by Anne Vuagnoux, Julien Blaine, Sarah Kéryna, Frédérique Guétat-Liviani and Liliane Giraudon.

ISBN: 978-1-937658-81-6

Design and typesetting by Kit Schluter

Collages by Frédérique Guétat-Liviani

Cataloging-in-publication data is available
from the Library of Congress

Distributed by the University Press of New England
One Court Street
Lebanon, NH 03766
www.upne.com

Nightboat Books
New York
www.nightboat.org

contents

but it's a long way

a departure   a departure of friends   anonymous ones   we can't

go back again   it's been crossed   we tried everything   to break the silence

it's also the beliefs   a beyond   where the loved ones   will come

help us   the communion   with them   to find the disappeared

there are prayers   these are   gestures   speaking   yet   there's a wall

words   sometimes   they're walls   with those prayers   we move beyond them

in the same language   we all have   a different definition   of the same word

language   locks us inside the words   not love   yes

there're people working   to bring them down   the walls

those who build them   aren't very many   but strong us too   when we're tired   when we haven't slept well

we build them   walls   we shut ourselves inside them

10   on the news   they speak of refugees   i can't watch   i'm too

disturbed   they're fleeing their country   the refugees   they're fleeing suffering

they find themselves   behind barbed wire   i can't watch

i don't pray often   it's rare that i pray

when i see images like that   i pray   right away   it's immediate

i think i can do that   pray

my mother   she was   a good person

the walls   make me think   of autism too

i worked at montfavet   autistics   are people who have so

much suffering   it prevents them from   reincarnating

reincarnation   it's become obvious to me   when i was 14 years old

it was hard   to work there   hard to feel oneself   powerless

one brought   what one could   every day   **11**

some carers   they were   like angels   but not all

i didn't build   a wall   to protect myself

we need sun   but not the sun that burns us

when i was small   i lived in the neighborhood   at 20   i left

i was a dreamer   i came back   to live here

i came   to france   the suburbs   in 1964   i

worked   in construction   before construction   for 4 or 5 months

12   in agriculture   i was born in morocco   in rabah

it's the period   of de gaulle   houses   cars

shops   it's wide open   now   it's closed

the borders   closed   there's no more   trust

in morocco   i am no longer   at home   i'll go back   in a box

now   i am   retired   i stay   home

between the old   and the young   there is a border

16 years in champfleury   12 years there   4 years there   the neighborhood   it's

good   but the people   i don't get on well   with

the people   who don't speak kindly   my son is gentle   he cries

the others hit him   here   i arrived young   with my

husband   we couldn't find a house   we found a garage for 3 months   we slept in the garage   i was pregnant   after we found

a h.l.m.   it's hard for me   to talk about it   that's where   mom

she died   dad lives here all alone   i'm the eldest   i was born   13

in france   in 77   the following year   we went back   to live in

algeria   i'm the only one with   french papers

papers   are a border   between brothers and sisters

what i'd really like   is to move   but the cost of rent

it's too high   that too   is a border

it's hard   to break them   the walls   what can we do

there are conflicts   sometimes   it's for a   plot of land

in africa   the borders   they are forgotten   when   it's

to judge a president   and then later   they are put back   to prevent

people from crossing   me   it's for love   that i left

i followed   my love   the shock here   it's when
i went   to church   for the first time   no one
14   came   to sit   next to me
now   i go   to another church
in the ivory coast   when a muslim dies   catholic men go
to his funeral   when it's a catholic   who dies   the muslims
go to the church   in france   the laws   poison things

i don't like for my son   to disrespect   the elders
in africa   you say   i made food for everyone   so everyone
eats   teaching your children   to do the dishes   it's not
exploitation   it's transmission

i live back there   for 14 years   no 15   since i am 15 years old

the projects   for people   it's synonymous   with scum

that's why   people don't want   to come   there's scum   **15**

everywhere   it's education   whether you're from a neighborhood   or a village

it's education   maybe   people could be brought here   to show

them   we're not   like that

in my section   there are   spaniards   moroccans

algerians   french people   for 11 years   i've been living in this section

we don't have problems   among us   before   i was   in

the other building   it was the same   i'm from morocco   the center of morocco

when i said   good-bye   to my parents   in front of the door   to the house

there   i crossed it   the border   my children   their language   it's french

now   i think in both languages   i count in french

even   in my head   later   between my children   and my parents

there will be another border   it will be language

it's because of the fence   water passes through the fence   it makes a shadow
and it makes sun   water   it isn't hard   it can pass

16 through the fence   there are men   in the water who die   after
they won't   die anymore   they will live

people flee they're looking for peace   but where they come from   there is
unemployment   poverty   if it were possible   to save someone
to open the door   to close it again   against the danger   before
there were no borders   no passports   no papers
i arrived   i was 23   i was too timid   i didn't speak
after i spoke   openly   as though i were crossing the border

my father   he   crossed it   the border   in 37

to escape   franco   he had brothers   in algeria   he went there

he learned arabic   my mother   she only spoke spanish

they died   i was small   6 years old   i was placed   in the orphanage

in avignon   after   i was called up   in algeria   it was war

but since i was   a breadwinner   yes for my sister   breadwinner

i soon came back   demobilized   in marseille   i worked as a

driver   i met a girl   from marseille   when she got pregnant

we had to get married   i wasn't of age   i was a ward of the nation   we

asked for   a permit   from the president   of the republic

later with my sister   we went to spain   to almeria   to see if

our grandfather's   sheepfold   was still there   we were watched

by the civic guard   we were told   there's nothing left   for the children

of republicans   my own children   have never been to spain

every morning   i go to the community center   to make coffee
to meet people   before that i took care   of collecting food
18   it was for soup kitchens   i also go to the secours populaire   to
collect   school supplies   at the start of the school year   and the rest of the time
for food   and baby care   the border   between wealthy
people   and poor people   that's the one   i look after
even   if i didn't know them   it's what i have left
of the political awareness   of my parents

it's language   french   it's been 10 months   actually before   i learned
french   but after i was   and i forgot   french
i stayed 14 years in   my children were born in   we left

because of the crisis no more work for my husband my husband was born in
he always lived in   but he speaks french well   because he goes out
with friends   me i stay   home   it's harder   to
learn to speak   my nationality   it allows me to live in france
i want to speak french   i want to work   i live there
on the 7th floor   the elevator is broken   it's been 3 months   but here
i feel good   where i was before   the people   weren't kind
i lived   with family   really   i'm better off here   next
week   i'm going back   to see my brother   don't put
the names   of places   and people   to avoid   my being recognized

you can't cross   because of the wall   otherwise   you'll run into it

there   on the other hand   you can cross   there's a hole in a wall   and there   a fence

20   you climb the fence   but if you don't know how to climb   what do you do

when there is   a river   you can make a bridge   everyone

can go   to the other side   and walk

school   it is at the edge   of our neighborhoods

we meet less often   when places   are not bordering

it's been 6 years   that i've been living in the neighborhood   there were some tense

periods   and then   the border   became a bit diluted

i've been working at the collège   for 7 years   i teach   technology

i try   to give   tools   to the children   they are handicapped by the

poverty of their vocabulary   it's a real handicap   but what's most important

for me   is to prove to them   that they are capable   of making it

when the new gymnasium   was built   someone wrote   on the wall
of the building   full of mistakes   *i wanna work   at citi hull*
at the bus stop   another one wrote   *here   it's the laaw of silence*   because
in this zone   there is   another law   the 2 a's of *laaw*   must be for that

i live on the border   between monclar   and champfleury   i am
a border dweller   by birth   born in algeria   on the moroccan border
my grandparents   were from morocco   but us   we felt algerian
my first name   my parents gave it to me   in homage   to the algerian
president   we were run out in 75   the army woke us   at 4 in the morning
we were allowed to take   a blanket with us   the women on one truck
with the children   the men   on another truck

in algeria   i wasn't schooled   i was with the animals
it was good   my grandparents looked after me   i collected the almonds
i took care of the chicken coop   repatriated to morocco   my parents schooled me
because of my first name   the schoolmaster   hit my fingers   all
morning long   with a palm branch   in the afternoon   i ran away

for 2 years   we lived all 5 of us   in a single room

it became impossible   my father   who worked in france

found a place   to bring us here

they bought me   shoes   for the first time

my father was a farm worker   his employer was a very   good man

he was the mayor of the village   without a title   my sister today

is a town councilor   in the same village

when we arrived   it was the month of march   i didn't know a word of french

i learned very quickly   by repeating   the words i heard

my brothers and sisters born in algeria   were like me   at school   they always

wanted   to be head of the class   an invisible border   turned

my young brothers   born in france   away from culture

i have an illness   diabetes   it's the illness   of the in-between

one is never   at the right place   at the right time

my border-dweller   illness

19 years in france   5 at monclar   i come from teaz   not far
from nador   i left   at age 14   with my parents
i was happy to leave   we arrived   at porto vecchio
it's expensive   life   in corsica   my husband   found work   here
my children   all 3   they were born here   my life   is here

i come from the same village as najat   in algeria   i arrived in
france   2 years ago   i didn't speak any french at all   if i speak
french well   it's thanks to najat   my father speaks french   well
because his mother   she was born in france   then she got married   to
an algerian   over there   my father he   was born in algeria
he got married   to my mother   in algeria also   they left
for the south   in ghardaïa   what was i saying   oh yes

in ghardaïa   it wasn't working out   there were family   problems   so
we left   we settled in algiers   but we had to leave again   because
my father's mother   she fell ill   my little brother was born there
and after we left again   for algiers   it wasn't working out again
that's why   we filled out the papers   my mother said   got to go far away

and   we arrived   in avignon

we moved in   to my uncle's   for 2 months   not even

24   but with the family   it still wasn't going well   my father found work

and an apartment   it's there   on the 9th floor   a two-room flat

i sleep   with my big sister   we are 4 children

my mother is pregnant   with the baby   that will make 5

my big sister is 19   my little brother is 8   the youngest is 3   that's her

within a year   my grandmother   she called   she said   here we are

so we went to pick up   my grandfather and my grandmother   at marignane

they moved in   to my uncle's   but another day   my grandmother

called my father again   come get us   your brother wants to hit your father

that's when they came   to live with us   it caused trouble   with my uncle

my grandfather   became sick   when he was 70 my father   right now   he is   in algeria   to bury my

grandfather   the timing is bad   my father had an accident   at work

when my grandfather   got sick   it's my father   who looked after him   **25**

to the end   he changed him   he washed him   he cared for him

i was afraid of coming to france   but i found najat   i found a friend

now i would be afraid   to leave   to leave her here   i would just like

to travel   yes   travel and come back   to her

they can pass   there is a door   but it's closed

locked shut   you can make a hole   in the wall   on the other side

of the wall   there is a house   and a garden you have to be aware   of misery   misery brings

anger   revolt   if everyone stays locked inside himself   if everyone has

26 his own personal wall   it's no good   it has to be destroyed   this wall

the demarcation line   is the one that prevents   from going elsewhere

it's been 40 years   since i've been living   in the neighborhood   i am a member of

the association   of renters   we fought a lot   against rent increases

to bring the expenses down   for rat control   there are believers

non-believers   we have to come together to fight   right now   we

are circulating   a petition   for the replacement

of the wastewater   column   crossing the border   this idea

my father passed it on to me   picked up by the s.t.o   he escaped 4 times

denounced by a schoolmate   he joined the f.f.i   my grandfather

he was a socialist   my father   after the war   he became a firefighter

his hatred of collaborators   he held on to it for a long time

life is good   outside   but   with the children   it's
hard   life is expensive   almost 10 years   since i've been
here across from the school   there is some concern   with the school   but

the place where i live   is calm   at school   there are children
and moms   who say swear words   in front of the others   i have 2 children
my daughter is 7 years old   my son is 4   before i was   at brive la gaillarde and
before that   in morocco   i came here at age 16   i only spoke arabic   french
i learned it   here   with my children   i only speak in french
they understand arabic   but they don't know how to speak it   with my husband
we speak 3 languages   we are berber   in morocco   at home
we spoke berber   at school   we spoke arabic

my parents   when they decided to leave   me i was crying

we took the car   two days of travel   we crossed spain

28   we were 5 children   another one was born later   7 in the van

my father was already working in france   he was working at the factory   now

he is retired   he returned to live   in morocco   but he comes back to see us

all the time   when they are older   i will teach

my children   to write in arabic   i didn't want to leave morocco

but   now   it's hard   to go back

i go there in the winter   when it's less hot   my husband   it's been 8 years

since he doesn't go anymore   he works at the factory   at the food processing plant

i'm looking for work   i can't find any   i have the permit   but no car

as a result   i stay home   otherwise   it causes trouble   with

the neighbors   i have a friend   in châteaurenard   she comes

to the house   every friday   she doesn't have children   mine

are hers   when i'm old   i'll do like my father

i'll live between both countries   i need both

every summer   i cross spain   the economic crisis   there
it's very serious   i arrived here   i was 8 years old   at school   in
morocco   i had learned several words   of french   but at home
we spoke arabic   before leaving   my parents warned me
i said good-bye   to everyone   my father was an electrician
he had left before us   he was already working here   now my father   he's retired

when i arrived at school   i was made fun of   but i made myself
a friend   he gave me candies   we didn't leave one another after that
at first   both of us   we spoke together   in sign language
at home   we spoke   arabic   at his home   turkish   together in french
after 2 months   i spoke well   it's been 9 years now
last year   he returned   to live in turkey   we grew up
like brothers   i miss him   i would like to see him again

i want to be a general practitioner   it's thanks to my sister   that i want

to be a doctor   my sister   all this time   she's wanted to be a doctor

30   my cousins they were born in france when they go to morocco they are laughed at

my little brother too   was born here   among brothers and sisters

we speak french   with my mother arabic   with my father both

i have good grades at school   the others are jealous   because

i'm a bledard   school   is the survival of the fittest   every man for himself

i do   ground fighting   i wear the colors of france   i have

dual citizenship   i loathe soccer   running after a ball

earning millions   a dog can do that   other people

who do   extraordinary   things   no one's gonna talk about it

one evening in morocco   i was a child   i got lost   a homeless person

took me in   what he had earned   begging that day   he spent it to

give me food   the next day   he found my house   he took me

back to my father   now   i live at la reine jeanne

2 days ago   a man died   of old age   we were all there   to say good-bye to him

my little brother   i let him play outside in the neighborhood   it's the only place

where i'm not worried   the dealers themselves   they want

to protect us   so we don't become like them   they look out for us

in the summer   when we go away   they watch the houses   since they were

born   they've lived outside   no one   to take care of them

when they grow up   they regret it   they say so   i find it sad

sometimes   there are even wars   because of   the separations

there are also   the borders you can't see   between arabs and

the racist french   it comes   from generalization   the terrorists

they say you have to kill   in the name of islam   so people believe

all muslims   are like that   but there's also racism

on the part of   maghrebians   toward   others

i am albanian   i'm 14 years old   i'm muslim   it doesn't show
when i'm alone   people don't give me funny looks   for example
at the supermarket checkout   when i'm not buying much
i ask   if i can go   ahead of the full shopping carts   i'm told yes
but when   i'm with my aunt   she wears a scarf
they don't let us pass   the eyes are cold   i think that
religion   it's something personal   it shouldn't   trace borders
albanians   from kossovo   suffered a lot   my older sister who's 17
she doesn't wear the veil   she has plenty of time   i feel french
with origins from elsewhere   when i was small   we moved
a lot   we were never able   to stop worrying   and then
when we learned   that my aunt was here   we came

i'm a bit pessimistic   for the future   there will be   more and more
refugees   maybe there will be   a 3rd world war   i'm afraid
of the future   now in kossovo   a false calm reigns   the other time   **33**
there was a match   between   albania and serbia   a toy flew over the stadium
a small remote control helicopter   with an albanian flag   the flag fell
onto the pitch   a serbian tore up the flag   so   the albanians
fought   against the serbians   my dream   would be to create
a movement   to help people   to open their eyes   being kind
being mean   it's a choice   it has nothing to do   with origins

in kossovo   when you come from the same village   everyone has the   same name
even if we're not   related   i find that beautiful
we're not required   to be from the same family   to feel solidarity

it's an end   the end of something   the beginning of something else

there is another beginning   the other day   we were in chlef   we went

34   to maghnia   at the border   where people   exchange

goods   with those   on the other side   the houses had

hot colors   we went on a whim   just to see

i have family in morocco   i've never seen them   on mom's side

we are from chlef   and algiers   from bab-el-oued   on dad's side

from oujda   they are algerians   but also moroccans   and also catalans   my

great-grandfather   he came from barcelona   my great-aunt   she lives in

barcelona   we speak on the telephone   i speak arabic and french

i'm learning english and spanish   i'm quite good   at spanish my ancestors are here   my great-grandfather   he arrived in marseille

he settled down in avignon   to work   my great grandfather was born

in algeria   he came here   in 63   my dad was born here

mom   in chlef   the first time she came   she was 6 months old

she left   she came back when she was 4   she left again   she came back at 19

my parents speak together in the 2 languages   they speak to me in the 2 languages

my first language   is french   then the arabic language   got

the upper hand   now   it's balanced out again   i got back yesterday

from algeria   it was too hot   it had been 3 years   since i hadn't been back

in marseille too   i have family   in la castellane   in consolat   in la belle de mai

here   in the area   i have my 2 grandmothers   in chlef   there's a whole area

it's just my family   i'd really like to put here   all the people i like in chlef

and in chlef   all the people that i like here   i'm a bit torn   over there

i like the landscapes   the countryside   the chickens   the cows   the sheep to tell you the truth   i prefer marseille   to avignon   but i also like   avignon

because   avignon   is my city   i feel good at monclar

36   at the end of every story   there is   a new story   me

i feel like   i grew up too fast

we hate one another   because we don't speak   the same language

sometimes   we can hate one another   because of the attacks

we don't know each other well   when we don't speak   the same language

the rivers   the seas   they're borders   in truth

i'd like to go to china   i'd like to go to peking

i go to mayotte   from time to time   but it's a long way

there are bridges   i already crossed the border   of belgium
and the border   of england   my family   is in france
in england   in algeria   i was born in avignon   at urbain 5
those on my mother's side   live in england   my mother   she is originally from
there   but i don't talk to her much   in class   i don't have good grades
in english   on the other hand   when i speak with the english   i can manage
when playing   *clash of clan*   then   i manage well

once i went   to england   but it's expensive   you're better off living
in dunkerque   that way   you can work during the day   go home at night
on my father-in-law's side   i have family in algeria   i quite like avignon
but   i prefer marseille   because in marseille
there is a subway   with car wheels

the first day   when you go to school   you cross a border

after   it's everyday life   later   i'd really like

38   to cross   the borders of america   go all   over

sometimes borders   are between friends   when we argue

it blocks us   we withdraw   instead of moving forward

with adults   the border   it's the secrets they keep

for example   when someone dies   and also when

they don't want to say   what gift   they're going to give us

age   memory   words   that you don't know

that's what it is   their border

an argument   that could separate us

i was born in mayotte   i've been here   for 3 months   i'm in 8th grade

i left my little sister   my little brother   my father   i left with my mother

my other little brother   he   is in marseille   at my uncle's

my dream   was to see the eiffel tower   for real   but the trip was very very

long   when we arrived in paris   it was a friend of my mother's   who

brought us as far as the subway to go to the station to take the train i couldn't

see   the eiffel tower   i would like to return to paris   to see it

once in marseille   we spent the day   i was exhausted

completely exhausted   then   we left by car again   to go to my aunt's

mom's sister   here at monclar   while waiting to find   accommodation

it hurts me   to have left the twins   on the 16th   they turned 9

so far   i still haven't made any friends   there are those

who make fun   because   for my age   i'm small

the problem   is that over there   there were too many thugs   for example   if

you were from the city   called cavani   the rivals   those from m'gombani

they would come   they'd slaughter you   that's why my mother

she said   we had to leave   i'm a bit worried   for my father

my brother and my sister   the ones who stayed

here it's calm   we're looking for a house   if we don't find one   we'll go to marseille
or paris   i'd rather live   in a calm city
40   a peaceful city   like avignon

the french language   here   it runs in the veins   the people who live far away
they tell themselves   we don't speak well   we have to learn to speak well
the people here   don't realize   that it runs in their veins

i'd like to study medicine   if i can't   i'll join the army
in mayotte   i reread my notebooks at night   in the morning   i got up
at 5 o'clock   to review a bit   i didn't like koranic school
but what's good   is that i learned to read arabic   this year   between
spanish and arabic   i chose spanish   to know   a new language

right now   i often have headaches   noise gives me a headache
when i was in mayotte   the 6th grade classes   were named after flowers   the
7th   after authors   the 8th   i can't remember   in 9th grade   names of
european capitals   since i was in 7th grade rousseau   i looked the name up
on the internet   i read a bunch of things   on rousseau   on the education of
children   i even know   that his first name   was jean-jacques

abdelsam   michel-françois   michel   najat

rabiâa   leïla   ensar   mireille   souhail

odile   chloé   samira   boumedienne   lucas

najat   s   nadia   hayat   nasser

kassym 4 years old   samaar 7 years old   kaïna 7 and a half   fakri 9 and a half

july 11 16   july 12 16   july 26 16   july 27 16

granges d'orel   *champfleury*   *granges d'orel*   *champfleury*
monclar   *monclar*

late   morning   *late   afternoon*   *day's   end*
frédérique guétat-liviani   october 16   saint-ruf

notes on the text

Bledard, sometimes spelled with an acute accent on the e (é), broadly designates a person from the Maghreb, though it can specifically denote an immigrant to France of North African origin. Bledard can be negatively connoted and used as an insult. Derived from bled, a familiar term used in the Maghreb to denote a town, a village, a county.

H.L.M. —*habitation à loyer modéré*— refers to public or private rent-controlled housing in France.

F.F.I. —*Les forces françaises de l'intérieur* (French forces of the interior)— designates the consolidation, under this name, of the principal military resistance groups in WWII, beginning in December 1943. The group would eventually be dissolved by de Gaulle and its members absorbed into the military. (Source: *Dictionnaire historique de la résistance*, Robert Laffont, 2006)

Marignane is the old name of the Marseille Provence airport.

Montfavet is a mental health hospital located in Avignon.

Secours populaire is a French popular relief organization dedicated to fighting poverty and discrimination.

S.T.O. —*Le service de travail obligatoire* (compulsory work service)— refers to a series of laws implemented in 1942-1943 by the Vichy regime at the request of the occupying German authorities, and resulting in the forced dispatch of several hundred thousand French people to feed the Nazi labor force. France was the only European country to force its citizens into collaboration. (Source: *Encyclopaedia Universalis*)

mais ça fait loin

un départ   un départ d'amis d'anonymes   on pourra plus

revenir en arrière   c'est franchi   on a tout tenté   pour casser le silence

c'est aussi les croyances   un au-delà   où les aimés   vont venir

nous aider   la communion avec eux   pour retrouver les disparus

il y a les prières   ce sont   des gestes   des paroles   pourtant   y'a un mur

les mots   des fois   c'est des murs   avec ces prières-là   on passe par-dessus

dans la même langue   on a tous   une définition différente   du même mot

le langage   ça nous enferme dans les mots   pas l'amour   oui

y'a des gens qui œuvrent   pour les faire tomber   les murs

ceux qui les construisent   sont pas nombreux   mais forts nous aussi   quand on est fatigué   quand on a mal dormi

on en construit   des murs   on s'enferme dedans

48   aux actualités   ils parlent des réfugiés   je peux pas regarder   je suis trop

perturbée   ils fuient leur pays   les réfugiés   ils fuient la souffrance

ils se retrouvent   derrière des barbelés   je peux pas regarder

je prie pas souvent   c'est rare que je prie

quand je vois des images comme ça   je prie   tout de suite   c'est instantané

je crois que je peux faire ça   prier

ma mère   c'était   quelqu'un de bien

les murs   me font penser   à l'autisme aussi

j'ai travaillé à montfavet   les autistes   ce sont des gens qui ont tant

de souffrance   ça les empêche de   se réincarner la réincarnation   c'est devenu évident pour moi   quand j'ai eu 14 ans

c'était difficile   de travailler là   difficile de se sentir   impuissant

on apportait   ce qu'on pouvait   au quotidien

certains soignants   ils étaient   comme des anges   mais   pas tous

j'ai pas construit   de mur   pour me protéger

on a besoin du soleil   mais pas du soleil qui nous brûle

petite   je vivais dans le quartier   à 20 ans   je suis partie   j'étais rêveuse

je suis revenue   vivre ici

j'arrive   en france   en banlieue   en 1964   je

travaille   dans le bâtiment   avant le bâtiment   pendant 4 ou 5 mois

50 dans l'agriculture   je nais au maroc   à rabah

c'est l'époque   de de gaulle   les maisons   les voitures

les magasins   c'est tout ouvert   maintenant   c'est fermé

les frontières   c'est fermé   il y a plus   la confiance

au maroc   je suis plus   chez moi   j'y retournerai   dans la boîte

maintenant   je suis   à la retraite   je reste   à la maison

entre les vieux   et les jeunes   il y a la frontière

16 ans à champfleury   12 ans là   4 ans là   le quartier   il est

bien   mais les gens   je m'entends pas bien   avec

les gens   qui parlent pas gentiment   mon fils est doux   il pleure

les autres le frappent   ici   je suis arrivée jeune   avec mon

mari   on n'a pas trouvé de maison   on a trouvé un garage pendant 3 mois   on a dormi dans le garage   j'étais enceinte   après on a

trouvé un h.l.m.   j'ai du mal   à parler de ça   c'est là que   maman

elle est morte   papa vit tout seul ici   je suis l'aînée   je suis née   **51**

en france   en 77   l'année suivante   on est repartis   vivre en

algérie   je suis la seule à avoir   les papiers français

les papiers   c'est une frontière   entre frères et sœurs

ce que j'aimerais bien   c'est déménager   mais le prix des loyers

c'est trop cher   ça aussi   c'est une frontière

c'est dur   de les casser   les murs   qu'est-ce qu'on peut faire

il y a des conflits   des fois   c'est pour une parcelle

en afrique   les frontières   on les oublie   quand   c'est

pour juger un président   et puis après   on les remet   pour empêcher

les gens de passer   moi   c'est par amour   que je suis partie j'ai suivi   mon amour   le choc ici   c'est quand

je suis allée   à l'église   la première fois   personne

n'est venu   s'asseoir   près de moi

maintenant   je vais   dans une autre église

en côte d'ivoire   quand un musulman meurt   les hommes catholiques vont

à son enterrement   quand   c'est un catholique   qui meurt   les musulmans

vont à l'église   en france   les lois   enveniment les choses

je n'aime pas que mon fils   manque de respect   aux aînés

en afrique   on dit   j'ai cuisiné pour tout le monde   alors tout le monde

en mange   apprendre à faire la vaisselle   à ses enfants   c'est pas de

l'exploitation   c'est de la transmission

j'habite derrière   depuis 14 ans   non 15   puisque j'ai 15 ans

les cités   pour les gens   c'est synonyme   de racaille

c'est à cause de ça   que les gens veulent pas venir   les racailles   y en a   **53**

partout   c'est l'éducation   qu'on soit d'un quartier   ou d'un village

c'est l'éducation   peut-être   on pourrait faire venir les gens   leur

montrer   qu'on n'est pas   comme ça

dans ma montée   il y a des   espagnols   des marocains

des algériens   des français   ça fait 11 ans   que j'habite la montée

on n'a pas de   problèmes   entre nous   avant   j'étais   dans

l'autre bâtiment   c'était pareil   je suis du maroc   du centre   du maroc

quand j'ai dit   au revoir   à mes parents   devant la porte   de la maison

là   je l'ai passée la frontière   mes enfants   leur langue   c'est le français

maintenant   je pense dans les 2 langues   je compte en français

même   dans ma tête   plus tard   entre mes enfants   et mes parents

il y aura une autre frontière   ce sera la langue

c'est à cause du grillage   l'eau passe par le grillage   ça fait de l'ombre

et ça fait du soleil   l'eau   elle est pas dure   elle peut passer à

54 travers le grillage   il y a des bonhommes   dans l'eau qui meurent   après

ils vont   plus mourir   ils vont vivre

les gens fuient   ils cherchent la paix   mais là où ils viennent   il y a

le chômage   la pauvreté   si c'était possible   de sauver quelqu'un

d'ouvrir la porte   de la refermer   sur le danger   avant

il y avait pas de frontières   pas de passeports   pas de papiers

je suis arrivée   j'avais 23 ans   j'étais trop timide   je parlais pas

après j'ai parlé   franchement   comme si je passais la frontière

mon père   il l'a franchie   lui   la frontière   en 37
pour fuir   franco   il avait des frères   en algérie   il est parti là-bas
il a appris l'arabe ma mère   elle parlait que l'espagnol

ils sont morts   j'étais petit 6 ans   on m'a placé   à l'orphelinat
d'avignon   après   j'ai été appelé   en algérie   c'était la guerre
mais comme j'étais   soutien de famille   oui pour ma sœur   soutien de famille
je suis vite rentré   démobilisé   à marseille   j'ai travaillé comme
chauffeur   j'ai rencontré une fille   une marseillaise   quand elle a été enceinte
il a fallu qu'on se marie   j'étais pas majeur   j'étais pupille de la nation   on a
demandé   une autorisation   au président   de la république .

plus tard avec ma sœur   on est allés en espagne   à almeria   voir si
la bergerie   de notre grand-père   était encore là   on était surveillés
par la garde civile   on nous a dit   il y a plus rien   pour les enfants
des républicains   mes enfants à moi   ils sont jamais allés en espagne

tous les matins   je vais au centre social   préparer le café
pour rencontrer les gens   avant je me suis occupé   du ramassage alimentaire
56   c'était pour les restos du cœur   je vais aussi au secours populaire   pour le
ramassage   des fournitures scolaires   à la rentrée   et le reste du temps
pour l'alimentation   et le soin des bébés   la frontière   entre les gens
aisés   et les gens pauvres   c'est celle-là   dont je m'occupe
même   si je les ai pas connus   c'est ce qui me reste
de la conscience politique   de mes parents

c'est la langue   le français   ça fait 10 mois   enfin avant   j'ai appris
le français   mais après j'étais   et j'ai oublié   le français
je suis restée 14 ans en   mes enfants sont nés à   on est partis

à cause de la crise   plus de travail   pour mon mari   mon mari est né en
il a toujours vécu en   mais il parle bien le français   parce qu'il sort
avec des copains   moi je reste   à la maison   c'est plus difficile   pour
apprendre à parler   ma nationalité   elle me permet de vivre en france
je veux parler français   je veux travailler   j'habite là
au 7ème étage   l'ascenseur est cassé   ça fait 3 mois   mais ici
je me sens bien   où j'étais avant   les gens   étaient pas gentils
j'habitais   avec la famille   vraiment   je suis mieux ici   la semaine
prochaine   j'y retourne   pour voir mon frère   il faudra pas mettre
les noms   des endroits   et des gens   pour pas   qu'on me reconnaisse

'

on peut pas passer   à cause du mur   sinon   on va se cogner

là   par contre   on peut passer   il y a un mur troué   et là   un grillage

58   on grimpe au grillage   mais si on sait pas grimper   qu'est-ce qu'on fait

quand il y a   une rivière   on peut faire un pont   chacun

peut y aller   de l'autre côté   et marcher

l'école   elle est à la limite   de nos quartiers

on se rencontre moins   quand les lieux   sont pas frontaliers

ça fait 6 ans   que j'habite le quartier   il y a eu des périodes tendues

et puis   la frontière   s'est un peu diluée

je travaille au collège   depuis 7 ans   j'enseigne   la technologie

j'essaie de donner   des outils   aux enfants   ils sont handicapés par la

pauvreté de leur vocabulaire   c'est un vrai handicap   mais le plus important

pour moi   c'est de leur prouver   qu'ils sont capables   d'y arriver

quand le nouveau gymnase   a été construit   quelqu'un a écrit   sur le mur
du bâtiment   avec plein de fautes   *je veu travaillé   a la mairi*
à l'arrêt de bus   un autre a écrit   *ici   c'est la loii   du silence*   parce que
dans cette zone   il y a   une autre loi   les 2 *i de loii*   ça doit être pour ça

je vis à la frontière   entre monclar   et champfleury   je suis
un frontalier   de naissance   né en algérie   à la frontière marocaine
mes grands-parents   étaient du maroc   mais nous   on se sentait algériens
mon prénom   mes parents me l'ont donné   en hommage   au président
algérien   on a été chassés en 75   l'armée nous a réveillés   à 4 heures du matin
on a eu le droit   d'emporter une couverture   les femmes dans un camion
avec les enfants   les hommes   dans un autre camion

en algérie   j'étais pas scolarisé   j'étais avec les bêtes
j'étais bien   mes grands-parents s'occupaient de moi   je ramassais les amandes
je m'occupais du poulailler   rapatriés au maroc   mes parents m'ont scolarisé
à cause de mon prénom   le maître d'école   m'a tapé sur les doigts   toute
la matinée   avec une branche de palmier   l'après-midi   je me suis enfui

pendant 2 ans   on a vécu tous les 5   dans une seule pièce

c'était plus possible   mon père   qui travaillait en france

a trouvé un logement   pour nous faire venir

on m'a acheté   des chaussures   pour la première fois

mon père était ouvrier agricole   son employeur était un homme   très bon

c'était le maire du village   sans étiquette   ma sœur aujourd'hui

est conseillère municipale   dans le même village

quand on est arrivés   c'était le mois de mars   je savais pas un mot de français

j'ai appris très vite   en répétant   les mots que j'entendais

mes frères et sœurs nés en algérie   étaient comme moi   à l'école   ils voulaient

toujours   être les premiers   une frontière invisible   a détourné

de la culture   mes jeunes frères   nés en france

j'ai une maladie   le diabète   c'est la maladie   de l'entre-deux

on n'est jamais   au bon endroit   au bon moment

ma maladie   de frontalier

19 ans en france   5 à monclar   je viens de teaz   juste à côté
de nador   je suis partie   à 14 ans   avec mes parents
j'étais contente de partir   on est arrivés   à porto vecchio
c'est cher   la vie   en corse   mon mari   a trouvé du travail   ici
mes enfants   les 3   ils sont nés ici   ma vie   elle est ici

je viens du même village que najat   en algérie   je suis arrivée en
france   il y a 2 ans   je parlais pas du tout français   si je parle
bien français   c'est grâce à najat   mon père parle bien   le français
parce que sa mère   elle est née en france   puis elle s'est mariée   avec
un algérien   là-bas   mon père lui   il est né en algérie
il s'est marié   avec ma mère   en algérie aussi   ils sont partis
dans le sud   à gardaïa   qu'est-ce que je disais   ah oui

à gardaïa   ça marchait pas trop   y avait des problèmes   de famille   alors
on est partis   on s'est installés à alger   mais il a fallu repartir   parce que
la mère de mon père   elle est tombée malade   mon petit-frère est né là
et après on est repartis   à alger   ça n'allait encore pas
c'est pour ça   qu'on a fait les papiers   ma mère a dit   faut partir loin

et   on est arrivés   à avignon

on s'est installés   chez mon oncle   pendant 2 mois   même pas

62 mais avec la famille   ça n'allait toujours pas   mon père a trouvé du travail

et un appartement   c'est là   au 9ème étage   un 2 pièces

je dors   avec ma grande sœur   on est 4 enfants

ma mère est enceinte   avec le bébé   ça fera 5

ma grande sœur a 19 ans   mon petit frère a 8 ans   la petite a 3 ans   c'est elle

au bout d'un an   ma grand-mère   elle a téléphoné   elle a dit   on est là

alors on est allés chercher   mon grand-père et ma grand-mère   à marignane

ils se sont installés chez mon oncle   mais un autre jour   ma grand-mère

elle a encore appelé mon père   viens nous chercher   ton frère veut frapper ton père

c'est là qu'ils sont venus   habiter chez nous   ça a fait des histoires avec mon tonton

mon grand-père   est tombé malade   à 70 ans

mon père   en ce moment   il est   en algérie   pour enterrer mon

grand-père   ça tombe mal   mon père a eu un accident   au travail

quand mon grand-père est tombé malade   c'est mon père   qui s'est occupé de lui

jusqu'au bout   il le changeait   il le lavait   il le soignait

j'avais peur de venir en france   mais j'ai trouvé najat   j'ai trouvé une amie

maintenant j'aurais peur   de m'en aller   de la laisser ici   j'aimerais juste

voyager   voilà   voyager et revenir   la retrouver

ils peuvent passer   il y a une porte   mais elle est fermée

à clef   on peut faire un trou   dans le mur   de l'autre côté

du mur   il y a une maison   et un jardin

il faut en prendre conscience   de la misère   la misère amène

la colère   la révolte   si chacun reste enfermé en lui-même   si chacun a

64 son mur personnel   ça va pas   il faut le détruire   ce mur

la ligne de démarcation   c'est elle qui empêche   d'aller ailleurs

ça fait 40 ans   que j'habite le quartier   je fais partie   de l'amicale

des locataires   on a beaucoup lutté   contre la hausse des loyers

pour faire baisser les charges   pour faire dératiser   il y a des croyants

des non-croyants   on doit s'unir pour lutter   en ce moment   on

fait circuler   une pétition   pour le remplacement

de la colonne   des eaux usées   franchir la frontière   cette idée

c'est mon père qui me l'a passée   embarqué au s.t.o   il s'est évadé 4 fois

dénoncé par un copain d'école   il a rejoint les f.f.i   mon grand-père

il était socialiste   mon père   après la guerre   il est devenu pompier

la haine des collabos   il l'a gardée longtemps

la vie est bien   dehors   mais   avec les enfants   c'est
difficile   la vie est chère   presque 10 ans   que je suis là
en face de l'école   il y a un peu de souci   avec l'école   mais

la place où j'habite   c'est calme   à l'école   il y a des enfants
et des mamans   qui disent des gros mots   devant les autres   j'ai 2 enfants
ma fille a 7 ans   mon fils a 4 ans   avant j'étais   à brive la gaillarde et
avant   au maroc   je suis venue à 16 ans   je parlais qu'arabe   le français
je l'ai appris   ici   avec mes enfants   je parle qu'en français
ils comprennent l'arabe   mais ils savent pas le parler   avec mon mari
on parle 3 langues   on est berbères   au maroc   à la maison
on parlait berbère   à l'école   on parlait arabe

mes parents   quand ils ont décidé de partir   moi je pleurais

on a pris la voiture   deux jours de voyage   on a traversé l'espagne

on était 5 enfants   un autre est né plus tard   7 dans la fourgonnette

mon père travaillait déjà en france   il travaillait à l'usine   maintenant

il est à la retraite   il est retourné vivre   au maroc   mais il revient nous voir

tout le temps   quand ils seront plus grands   j'apprendrai

à écrire l'arabe   à mes enfants   je voulais pas quitter le maroc

mais   maintenant   c'est dur   d'y retourner

j'y vais en hiver   quand il fait moins chaud   mon mari   ça fait 8 ans

qu'il y va plus   il travaille à l'usine   à l'usine agroalimentaire

je cherche du travail   je trouve pas   j'ai le permis   mais pas de voiture

du coup   je reste à la maison   sinon   ça fait des histoires   avec

les voisines   j'ai une amie   à châteaurenard   elle vient

à la maison   tous les vendredis   elle a pas d'enfants   les miens

c'est les siens   quand je vieillirai   je ferai comme mon père

je vivrai entre les 2 pays   j'ai besoin des 2

tous les étés   je traverse l'espagne   la crise économique   là-bas
elle est très grave   je suis arrivé ici   j'avais 8 ans   à l'école   au
maroc   j'avais appris quelques mots   de français   mais à la maison
on parlait arabe   avant de partir   mes parents m'ont prévenu
j'ai dit au revoir   à tout le monde   mon père était électricien
il était parti avant nous   il travaillait déjà ici   mon père maintenant   il est retraité

quand je suis arrivé à l'école   on s'est moqué de moi   mais je me suis fait
un ami   il m'a donné des bonbons   on s'est plus quittés
au début   tous les 2   on se parlait   la langue des signes
chez moi   on parlait   arabe   chez lui   turc   ensemble le français
au bout de 2 mois   je parlais bien   ça fait 9 ans maintenant
l'année dernière   il est retourné   vivre en turquie   on a grandi
comme des frères   il me manque   je voudrais le revoir

je veux être généraliste   c'est ma sœur   qui m'a donné envie

d'être médecin   ma sœur   depuis tout le temps   elle veut être médecin

68   mes cousins   ils sont nés en france   quand ils vont au maroc   on se moque d'eux

mon petit frère aussi   est né ici   entre frères et sœurs

on parle français   avec ma mère l'arabe   avec mon père les 2

j'ai de bons résultats scolaires   les autres sont jaloux   parce que

je suis un bledard   l'école   c'est la loi du plus fort   chacun pour soi

je fais   du combat au sol   je porte les couleurs de la france   j'ai la

double nationalité   je déteste le foot   courir derrière un ballon

gagner des millions   un chien peut le faire   d'autres gens qui

font des choses   extraordinaires   personne va en parler

un soir au maroc   j'étais enfant   je me suis perdu   un s.d.f

m'a recueilli   ce qu'il avait gagné   en mendiant la journée   il l'a dépensé pour

me donner à manger   le lendemain   il a retrouvé ma maison   il m'a

ramené chez mon père   maintenant   j'habite à la reine jeanne

il y a 2 jours un homme est mort de vieillesse on était tous là pour lui dire au revoir mon petit frère   je le laisse jouer dehors   dans le quartier   il y a que là

que je suis pas inquiet   les dealers eux-mêmes   ils veulent nous

protéger   pour qu'on devienne pas comme eux   ils font attention à nous   69

l'été   quand on part   ils surveillent   les maisons   depuis qu'ils sont

nés   ils ont vécu dehors   personne   pour s'occuper d'eux

quand ils sont grands   ils regrettent   ils le disent   je trouve ça triste

des fois   il y a même des guerres   à cause   des séparations

il y a aussi   les frontières qui se voient pas   entre   les arabes et

les français racistes   ça vient   de la généralisation   les terroristes

ils disent qu'il faut tuer   au nom de l'islam   alors on croit

que tous les musulmans   sont comme ça   mais y'a aussi du racisme

de la part   des maghrébins   vis-à-vis   des autres

je suis albanais   j'ai 14 ans   je suis musulman   ça se voit pas

quand je suis seul   les gens me regardent pas de travers   par exemple

70   à la caisse du supermarché   quand je prends pas grand-chose

je demande   si je peux passer   devant les caddies remplis   on me dit oui

mais quand   je suis avec ma tante   elle porte un foulard

on nous laisse pas passer   les regards sont froids   je crois que

la religion   c'est un truc personnel   ça doit pas   tracer des frontières

les albanais du kossovo   ont beaucoup souffert   ma grande sœur de 17 ans

elle porte pas le voile   elle a bien le temps   je me sens français

avec des origines d'ailleurs   quand j'étais petit   on a

beaucoup déménagé   on n'arrivait jamais   à se tranquilliser   et puis

quand on a appris   que ma tante était là   on est venus je suis un peu pessimiste   pour l'avenir   il y aura   de plus en plus   de

réfugiés   peut-être qu'il y aura   une 3ème guerre mondiale   j'ai peur

de l'avenir maintenant au kossovo   le faux calme règne   l'autre fois

y'a eu   un match   albanie serbie   un jouet a survolé le stade

un petit hélicoptère téléguidé   avec un drapeau albanais   le drapeau est tombé

sur le terrain   un serbe a déchiré le drapeau   alors   les albanais

se sont battus   contre les serbes   mon rêve   ce serait de créer

un mouvement   pour aider les gens   à ouvrir les yeux   être gentil

être méchant   c'est un choix   ça n'a rien à voir   avec les origines

au kossovo   quand on vient du même village   on porte tous le même nom

même si on n'est pas   apparentés   je trouve ça beau

on n'est pas obligés   d'être de la même famille   pour être solidaires

c'est une fin   la fin de quelque chose   le début d'autre chose
il y a un autre début   l'autre jour   on était à chlef   on est
72   partis à maghnia   à la frontière   là où les gens   échangent
des marchandises   avec ceux   de l'autre côté   les maisons avaient
des couleurs chaudes   on y est allés comme ça   juste pour voir

j'ai de la famille au maroc   je l'ai jamais vue   du côté de maman
on est de chlef   et d'alger   de bab-el-oued   du côté de papa
d'oujda   ils sont algériens   mais aussi marocains   et aussi catalans   mon
arrière-grand-père   il venait de barcelone   ma grand-tante   elle habite à
barcelone   on se parle au téléphone   je parle arabe et français
j'apprends l'anglais et l'espagnol   je suis plutôt forte   en espagnol

mes ancêtres sont ici   mon arrière-grand-père   il est arrivé à marseille

il s'est installé à avignon   pour travailler   mon grand-père est né

en algérie   il est venu ici   en 63   mon papa est né ici

maman   à chlef   la première fois qu'elle est venue   elle avait 6 mois

elle est repartie   elle est revenue à 4 ans   elle est repartie   elle est revenue à 19 ans

mes parents se parlent dans les 2 langues   ils me parlent dans les 2 langues

ma première langue   c'est le français   après la langue arabe   a pris

le dessus   maintenant   ça s'est rééquilibré   je suis revenue hier

d'algérie il faisait trop chaud   ça faisait 3 ans   que j'y étais pas retournée

à marseille aussi   j'ai de la famille   à la castellane   à consolat   à la belle de mai

ici   dans le quartier   j'ai mes 2 grands-mères   à chlef   y'a un quartier entier

c'est que ma famille   j'aimerais bien mettre ici   tous les gens que j'aime à chlef

et à chlef   tous les gens que j'aime ici   je suis un peu déchirée   là-bas

j'aime les paysages   la campagne   les poules   les vaches   les moutons

à vrai dire   je préfère marseille   à avignon   mais j'aime aussi   avignon
parce que   avignon   c'est ma ville   je me sens bien à monclar
74   à la fin de chaque histoire   il y a   une nouvelle histoire   moi
j'ai l'impression   d'avoir grandi trop vite

on se déteste   parce qu'on parle pas   la même langue
des fois   on peut se détester   à cause des attentats
on se connaît mal   quand on parle pas   la même langue
les rivières   les mers   c'est des frontières   en vérité
j'aimerais aller en chine   j'aimerais aller à pékin
je vais à mayotte   de temps en temps   mais ça fait loin

il y a des ponts   j'ai déjà passé la frontière   de la belgique

et la frontière   de l'angleterre   ma famille   elle est en france

en angleterre   en algérie   je suis né à avignon   à urbain 5

ceux du côté de ma mère   vivent en angleterre   ma mère   elle est originaire de

là   mais je parle pas beaucoup avec elle   en classe   j'ai pas de bonnes notes

en anglais   par contre   quand je parle avec les anglais   j'y arrive

en jouant à   *clash of clan*   là   je me débrouille bien

je suis allé une fois   en angleterre   mais c'est cher   il vaut mieux vivre

à dunkerque   comme ça   on peut travailler la journée   rentrer le soir

du côté de mon beau-père   j'ai de la famille en algérie   j'aime bien avignon

mais   je préfère marseille   parce qu'à marseille

il y a un métro   avec des roues de voiture

le premier jour   quand on rentre à l'école   on franchit une frontière
après   c'est la vie de tous les jours   plus tard   j'aimerais bien
76   franchir   les frontières de l'amérique   aller un peu   partout

des fois les frontières   c'est entre les copains   quand on se dispute
ça nous bloque   on recule   au lieu d'avancer

avec les adultes   la frontière   c'est les secrets qu'ils gardent
par exemple   quand quelqu'un meurt   et aussi quand
ils veulent pas dire   le cadeau   qu'ils vont nous faire
l'âge   la mémoire   les mots   qu'on connaît pas
c'est ça   leur frontière

une dispute   ça pourrait nous séparer

je suis né à mayotte   je suis là   depuis 3 mois   je suis en 4ème

j'ai quitté ma petite sœur   mon petit frère   mon père   je suis parti avec ma mère

mon autre petit frère   lui   il est à marseille   chez mon oncle

mon rêve   c'était de voir la tour eiffel   en vrai   mais le voyage était très très

long   quand on est arrivés à paris   c'est une amie de ma mère   qui nous a

amenés   jusqu'au métro   pour aller à la gare   prendre le train   j'ai pas pu

voir   la tour eiffel   je voudrais retourner à paris   pour la voir

arrivés à marseille   on est restés une journée   j'étais crevé

complétement crevé   ensuite   on est partis en voiture   chez ma tante

la sœur de maman   ici à monclar   en attendant de trouver   un logement

ça me fait mal   d'avoir laissé les jumeaux   le 16   ils ont eu 9 ans

pour l'instant   je me suis pas encore fait de copains   y en a qui

se moquent   parce que   pour mon âge   je suis petit de taille

le problème   c'est que là-bas   y avait trop de voyous   par exemple   si

t'étais de la ville   qui s'appelle cavani   les rivaux   ceux de m'gombani

ils venaient   ils te massacraient   c'est pour ça que ma mère

elle a dit   qu'il fallait partir   je suis un peu inquiet   pour mon père

mon frère et ma sœur   ceux qui sont restés

ici c'est calme   on cherche une maison   si on trouve pas   on ira à marseille
ou à paris   je préférerais vivre   dans une ville calme

une ville paisible   comme avignon

la langue française ici   elle coule dans les veines   les gens qui habitent loin
ils se disent   on sait pas bien parler   il faut qu'on apprenne à parler bien
les gens ici   se rendent pas compte   que ça coule dans leurs veines

j'aimerais faire médecine   si j'y arrive pas   je ferai l'armée
à mayotte   je relisais mes cahiers la nuit   le matin   je me levais
à 5 heures   pour réviser un peu   j'aimais pas l'école coranique
mais ce qui est bien   c'est que j'ai appris à lire l'arabe   cette année entre
l'espagnol et l'arabe   j'ai choisi l'espagnol   pour connaître   une nouvelle langue

en ce moment   j'ai souvent mal à la tête   le bruit me donne mal à la tête

quand j'étais à mayotte   les classes de 6ème   portaient des noms de fleurs   les

5ème   des noms d'auteurs   les 4ème   je sais plus   les 3ème   des noms de

capitales européennes   vu que j'étais en 5ème rousseau   j'ai cherché le nom

sur internet   j'ai lu plein de choses   sur rousseau   sur l'éducation des

enfants   je sais même   que son prénom   c'était jean-jacques

abdelsam   michel-françois   michel   najat

rabiâa   leïla   ensar   mireille   souhail

odile   chloé   samira   boumedienne   lucas

najat   s   nadia   hayat   nasser

kassym 4 ans   samaar 7 ans   kaïna 7 ans et demi   fakri 9 ans et demi

11 juillet 16   12 juillet 16   26 juillet 16   27 juillet 16

granges d'orel   *champfleury*   *granges d'orel*   *champfleury*
monclar   *monclar*

fin de matinée   *fin d'après-midi*   *fin de journée*
frédérique guétat-liviani   octobre 16   saint-ruf

contours and conditions of
but it's a long way

1. What are the contours of **but it's a long way**?

2. The text closes with the name of Jean-Jacques Rousseau. Then a recitative of the names of people whose words are transcribed. What importance does this nominal end-point hold for the text? And its proximity to the names of people who were approached?

3. What becomes of the author in proximity to these transcriptions?

4. The condition of **but it's a long way** is an accumulation of distances. The condition of speech is that of a proximity. What is the sense of this abyss? Is it an abyss?

5. **but it's a long way** is built in the breaches of walls, borders and barbed wire. The text seems to offer itself in counterpoint as a respiration. What is this architecture, for you, transcribing, for the body that attunes itself to this movement? What emotion?

What are the contours of but it's a long way?

but it's a long way was written following a series of encounters with
the inhabitants of three extra-mural projects in Avignon. The encounters
took place in the month of July 2016 while, intra-murally, as is the case
every year, the Festival d'Avignon was underway. Avignon is a small city,
the distances are short. Yet the ramparts encircling the old city seem
impassable. Festival goers remain inside. The inhabitants live on the
outside. A long time ago, I studied, inside. Later, I earned a living, outside.
An association called l'Antre Lieux invited us, Sarah Kéryna and myself,
to cross this demarcation line, at the height of summer. Liliane Giraudon
joined us in the fall.

For each encounter, the same protocol: a table, two chairs, facing one another,
a big ledger and several tracts mentioning the border as well as its crossing.
The whole thing set up at the foot of the residences.
Three different neighbourhoods, nonetheless similar, in the infinity of
the forbidden space.
The encounters happen in the open air but the space is closed, there is
silence around.

The contours cannot be written. They draw themselves, back-lit, against invisible screens.

Women, men, children, come to sit at my table. They speak, I write their words.

Always by hand, no recourse to some machine or other.

The slackening of the contour, its near effacement, this is the only cost at which the held views of the city can be transgressed.

The singular word then rises to the surface.

The contour of the words on the ledger render visible the time spent together, at the same table.

Visible are both the trembling bodies and time trembling.

The text closes on the name of Jean-Jacques Rousseau. Followed by a recitative of the names of people whose words are transcribed. What importance does this nominal outcome hold for the text? And its proximity to the names of those people who were approached?

Transcription is a gesture. A gesture does not have the finality of an action. By reproducing them, through writing, the names heard are transfigured. Without a portend as to their becoming. A name is heavy to carry. To transcribe it is to return to it a bit of its lightness. The same is true of the names of the projects. Often nicknamed rather than named, and subjected to the same fate as their inhabitants. They are not cited, they are spoken about. Thus, I copied out several formulas in the press. Common formulas for the inventory of the unnamed:

people of the projects, sensitive areas, disadvantaged people, undocumented, ineligible, clandestine, refugees, single-parent families, first-time offender, traffickers, job applicants, women in a precarious situation, radicalized youth, with suicidal tencencies, on parole, RSA* beneficiaries, unregistered at the Pôle emploi*, beneficiaries of the social minimum, drug addicted, protective residency, on the wait-list for social housing...

They are spoken of in the third person. A person who is absolutely non-existent, absent to herself or himself, outside of history without a past without a future. That society carries, like a weight. A weight is not named, it is only measurable. That is why I wanted to convoke all the heard voices. To call them by their own names, mixed with Rousseau's, the only author whose name was cited during these meetings. Rousseau, whose errancy accompanies that of the little boy from the Comoros, not long ago.

What becomes of the author alongside these transcriptions?

The author —it seems to me— is not erased. The author is allied to the others, through a silent pact. The words are not erased either. As soon as they are written down, they are displaced, organize themselves and dislocate. Ties are created, that had hitherto been discerned. It is certainly in the blanks, the spaces, that I am most present. I hold myself there because those who are speaking, speak to us so rarely. We who are saturated with discourses, information, commentaries. Placing space betwen their words is a way of keeping quiet, in order that they better be heard. To make things and facts be heard, to be the author of restitution. All the people encountered continually hesitated. They sometimes hesitated because of the French language, which was foreign to them. They hesitated at other times, not finding the word that suited them. They hesitated, carried away by their narrative, not knowing anymore where they were with it. Their hesitations suspended speaking and the body as well, in an unstable equilibrium on the office chairs we had placed on the dry lawn. The sentences were split wide open. I tried to retrieve these cracks in writing, in the rhythm of the line. Those who came to sit across from me were all so different, in terms of their age, their sex, their origins. But errancy was the thread that connected all of their narratives. I wanted to hold on to the evidence of this by not cutting that thread, by allowing it to spread out from one end to the other, like a streak. That is what I attempted to do, to retrieve the substance of interrupted speech, through the proliferation of cesurae. I remained there, suspended from the gesture of writing.

The condition of **but it's a long way** is an accumulation of distances. The condition of its speaking is that of a proximity. What is the sense of this abyss? Is it an abyss?

Élisée Reclus while drawing atlases would say: "one must definitively gain consciousness of our human solidarity, forming one body with the planet itself."

The distances have been travelled. They have imprinted themselves in the bodies that have come to a halt. All those who came to sit at my table, had travelled some road, a long road. That road is in them, in their bodies, in the body of their lineage. All of them are at a distance from a history, a family, a place, a memory. They have distanced themselves. *but it's a long way* is a halt. One must mark a pause, stop moving, to be able to speak of it, of the distance. To retrieve the inertia, resist walking, sit down a while. I don't think there is an abyss between the distance travelled and the words deposited there. The abyss is bottomless, one is voided there. *but it's a long way* is a receptacle for speech, the one receives, the other sets itself down. It's a hollow, a roundness that is in sharp contrast with the angular architecture of the projects encircling the table. It's like an inner hole that we are digging, without recourse to any tools other than language. Here, geographic distance is abolished.

but it's a long way is built inside the breaches of walls, borders and barbed wire. The text seems to offer itself as a counterpoint, as a respiration. What is this architecture, for you, transcribing, for the body attuned to this movement? What emotion?

> *"these lines speak [...] of a passage over that which is read to the point of bleeding, to the point of the wound."*
>
> —Jacques Derrida*

Writing is an enterprise that tends to unwall. It enters into the walls, turns them over, they become the support for that which they had a mission to prevent.

Behind those, there is the multitude of lives. Through the gaps of writing, one discerns the layering of voices that emerge from them. In the entanglement, they rise but one doesn't cover over the others. They nest in one another, contradict, and question one another. The walls against which they have collided, the wire on which some have been torn, have left holes, gashes. The leafing of voices has allowed words to migrate, from one narrative to another.

They escape in the line spacing, one retrieves them later, articulated and transformed, in other mouths. The voices of *but it's a long way* incorporate silence. Emotion is not pronounced. Sometimes the blanks are inscribed as a sign of mourning, sometimes as a sign of the unheard of. They are never ornaments. They are not intermissions, there are no acts. There are gestures. Speaking is a gesture similar to the one that stitches the snag. It is in order to exceed the impossibility of speaking that one enters inside. By following the passage where the walls that formed one body have eroded. At that precise place where the human meets the other.

The repetition of flight plunges into shock. The space of the text is that archive. In the incessant movement between here and elsewhere, the words exchanged become the auxiliary of displacement. Writing is a way to give substance to those whose lives were spoliated.

Well before their arrival in the world.

RSA: Revenue de solidarité active/Active solidarity income: The purpose of the RSA is to "guarantee its receipients sufficient means for living, in order to combat poverty, encourage the exercise of or return to professional activity and assist in the social integration of recipients" (Law no2008-1249 of December 1, 2008). From information provided by the Insee (National Institute of Statistics and Economic Studies), France.

Pôle emploi: employment agency. This French governmental agency has as its mission to register unemployed people, provide opportunities to find work, and provide financial aid.

Quote from Jacques Derrida on p. 89 tr. Joshua Wilner and Thomas Dutoit, modified.

Born in Grenoble in 1963, FRÉDÉRIQUE GUÉTAT-LIVIANI makes installations that speak of languages, and writes texts that she builds like images. A founding member of the artists' collective Intime Conviction (1988–94), she is now the publisher of Fidel Anthelme x. The author of several collections of poetry, she is of the caste neither of poets nor of artists. Instead, she inhabits a space in-between. She lives in Marseille.

NATHANAËL is the author of more than thirty books written in English or in French and published in the United States, Québec and France. Her translations include works by Catherine Mavrikakis, Édouard Glissant, Hervé Guibert, Reginald Gibbons, and Hilda Hilst (the latter in collaboration with Rachel Gontijo Araújo). Nathanaël lives in Chicago.

NIGHTBOAT BOOKS

Nightboat Books, a nonprofit organization, seeks to develop audiences for writers whose work resists convention and transcends boundaries. We publish books rich with poignancy, intelligence, and risk. Please visit nightboat.org to learn more about us and how you can support our future publications.

The following individuals have supported the publication of this book. We thank them for their generosity and commitment to the mission of Nightboat Books:

Elizabeth Motika
Benjamin Taylor

In addition, this book has been made possible, in part, by a grant from the National Endowment for the Arts and the New York State Council on the Arts Literature Program.

Traverser *passer* franchir essayer **rallier**

rejoindre venir se rendre *se faufiler* s'effacer

transiter *changer* disparaître ***marcher*** s'en aller

fuir *quitter*

se glisser laisser tenter

Traverser *passer* franchir essayer **rallier**

rejoindre venir se rendre *se faufiler* s'effacer

transiter *changer* disparaître ***marcher*** s'en aller

fuir *quitter*

se glisser laisser tenter

La lisière **au bord** *le mur*

la séparation au bout la frontière la ligne de démarcation

à la fin la limite **la bordure**

de l'autre côté *à l'extrémité*

La lisière **au bord** *le mur*

la séparation au bout la frontière la ligne de démarcation

à la fin la limite **la bordure**

de l'autre côté *à l'extrémité*